Dear Parent:
Your child's love of reading st...

Every child learns to read in a different way and at his or her own speed. Some go back and forth between reading levels and read favorite books again and again. Others read through each level in order. You can help your young reader improve and become more confident by encouraging his or her own interests and abilities. From books your child reads with you to the first books he or she reads alone, there are I Can Read Books for every stage of reading:

SHARED READING
Basic language, word repetition, and whimsical illustrations, ideal for sharing with your emergent reader

BEGINNING READING
Short sentences, familiar words, and simple concepts for children eager to read on their own

READING WITH HELP
Engaging stories, longer sentences, and language play for developing readers

READING ALONE
Complex plots, challenging vocabulary, and high-interest topics for the independent reader

ADVANCED READING
Short paragraphs, chapters, and exciting themes for the perfect bridge to chapter books

I Can Read Books have introduced children to the joy of reading since 1957. Featuring award-winning authors and illustrators and a fabulous cast of beloved characters, I Can Read Books set the standard for beginning readers.

A lifetime of discovery begins with the magical words "I Can Read!"

Visit www.icanread.com for information
on enriching your child's reading experience.

I Can Read!

BEGINNING 1 READING

Pinkalicious®
and the Pink Parakeet

To Brigitte, with love

The author gratefully acknowledges
the artistic and editorial contributions of
Dynamo, Loryn Brantz, Kirsten Berger, and Natalie Engel.

I Can Read Book® is a trademark of HarperCollins Publishers.

Pinkalicious and the Pink Parakeet
Copyright © 2015 by Victoria Kann

PINKALICIOUS and all related logos and characters are trademarks of Victoria Kann. Used with permission.

Based on the HarperCollins book *Pinkalicious* written by
Victoria Kann and Elizabeth Kann, illustrated by Victoria Kann
All rights reserved. Printed in the United States of America.
No part of this book may be used or reproduced in any manner whatsoever without
written permission except in the case of brief quotations embodied in critical articles and reviews.
For information address HarperCollins Children's Books, a division of HarperCollins Publishers,
195 Broadway, New York, NY 10007.
www.icanread.com

Library of Congress Control Number: 2014949455

ISBN 978-0-06-224596-0 (trade bdg.) —ISBN 978-0-06-224597-7 (pbk.)

16 17 18 PC/WOR 10 9 8 7 6 5 4 3 2
❖
First Edition

I Can Read!

BEGINNING 1 READING

Pinkalicious®
and the Pink Parakeet

by Victoria Kann

It was Bird Week at school,
my favorite week ever!
Every day my class
learned fun facts about birds.

I told my family everything I learned.

"Fact," I told Mommy.

"Hummingbirds can fly backward."

"Fact," I told Daddy.

"Robin eggs are blue."

"Fact," I told Peter.

"Orioles can eat

seventeen worms in a minute."

"Big whoop," he said.

"So can I."

The last day of Bird Week
was the best one yet.

My class went on a field trip
to the house of birds at the zoo!

On the bus,

I took out my bird book.

I flipped through the pages

and saw something amazing.

"Fact," I cried.

"There's a pink parakeet!
It's small and sweet
and pinkerrifically pink!"

"Yes," said Ms. Penny,

"but it's a very rare bird.

You may not see one today."

I wasn't so sure about that.

I was really good at bird-watching.

When we got to the house of birds,

I couldn't believe my eyes.

I saw one red parrot,

two blue peacocks,

six green-and-yellow lovebirds,

and a toucan with an orange beak.

But not a single pink parakeet.

Soon it was time to leave.

"I'm sorry, Pinkalicious,"
Alison said.

"Maybe you'll see one another day."

We started walking out together,
but just as we got to the door,
I heard a strange call.
"Pink, pink, pink, PINK!"

"What was that?" I said.

"Pink, pink, pink, PINK!"

Alison and I looked at each other.

"The parrot!" we cried.

We ran over to the parrot's perch.

"He's telling us something," I said.

The parrot lifted its wing.

It was pointing to the door.

"Pink, pink, pink, PINK!" it called.

A pink parakeet!

At last, I saw one.

It was right inside

Ms. Penny's hood!

"Wait, Ms. Penny!"
I called.
But she was already
out the door.

By the time we caught up to
Ms. Penny, it was too late.

Her hood was empty.

The bird was gone.

22

I was so upset.

I told Ms. Penny what happened.

"Maybe it didn't fly far," she said.

Together, the whole class searched

for the missing pink parakeet.

23

Everyone scanned the treetops,

but the leaves were too thick.

We looked through the bushes,

but we didn't see a thing.

I was about ready to give up

when I remembered my bird book.

I read about the parakeet again

and came up with a plan.

"'Fact,'" I read out loud.

"'Pink parakeets eat fruit.'

Who has a snack?"

Molly had cherries from lunch.

"'Fact,'" I said.

"'They also like taking baths.'"

Jack filled a small dish with water.

We put everything together.

"There's one last fact," I said.

"These parakeets tweet a lot.

So here goes . . . !"

I closed my eyes
and thought pink thoughts.
Then I whistled my very best
pinkerrific birdcall.

Suddenly, I heard wings flapping.

My classmates gasped.

I opened my eyes, and there it was!

The pink parakeet was eating fruit

while taking a bath.

Ms. Penny picked up
the parakeet gently
and brought it back to the birdhouse.
The whole class cheered!

When she came back, Ms. Penny laughed.

"Pinkalicious saved the day," she said.

"And that's a fact!"